Cook Memorial Public Library

3 1122 01510 8496

SEP 1 2 2018

S0-BCQ-993

Principals

Julie Murray

COOK MEMORIAL LIBRARY DISTRICT
413 N. MILWAUKEE AVE.
LIBERTYVILLE, ILLINOIS 60048

Abdo Kids Junior
is an Imprint of Abdo Kids
abdopublishing.com

Abdo
Kids

MY COMMUNITY: JOBS

abdopublishing.com

Published by Abdo Kids, a division of ABDO, P.O. Box 398166, Minneapolis, Minnesota 55439.
Copyright © 2019 by Abdo Consulting Group, Inc. International copyrights reserved in all countries.
No part of this book may be reproduced in any form without written permission from the publisher.
Abdo Kids Junior™ is a trademark and logo of Abdo Kids.

Printed in the United States of America, North Mankato, Minnesota.

052018

092018

 THIS BOOK CONTAINS
RECYCLED MATERIALS

Photo Credits: iStock, Shutterstock

Production Contributors: Teddy Borth, Jennie Forsberg, Grace Hansen

Design Contributors: Christina Doffing, Candice Keimig, Dorothy Toth

Library of Congress Control Number: 2017960555

Publisher's Cataloging-in-Publication Data

Names: Murray, Julie, author.

Title: Principals / by Julie Murray.

Description: Minneapolis, Minnesota : Abdo Kids, 2019. | Series: My community: Jobs |
    Includes glossary, index and online resources (page 24).

Identifiers: ISBN 9781532107900 (lib.bdg.) | ISBN 9781532108884 (ebook) |
    ISBN 9781532109379 (Read-to-me ebook)

Subjects: LCSH: School principals--Juvenile literature. | Teachers and community--Juvenile literature. |
    Occupations--Careers--Jobs--Juvenile literature. | Community life--Juvenile literature.

Classification: DDC 371.2012--dc23

Table of Contents

Principals

Lou is a principal. He works for a school.

They do many things. Jane gets
kids on the bus.

They are school leaders.

Evan gives a high five.

They work with teachers.

They work with parents.

13

They work with students.

Dana helps in the classroom.

They have meetings.

Alex listens to the parents.

They have an office. John looks over the school budget.

Kate  being a principal.

A Principal's Tools

budget calculator

computer

keys

a school!

Glossary

enjoy
to find joy in.

budget
a plan for how much money will be spent and earned during a certain period.

leader
a person who makes important decisions for and helps lead a group.

Index

Abdo Kids
ONLINE
FREE! ONLINE MULTIMEDIA RESOURCES

Visit **abdokids.com** and use this code to access crafts, games, videos, and more!

Abdo Kids Code:
MPK7900